Labour's Extreme Neoliberalism

This book is dedicated to the memory of my beloved partner Nick Nuttgens, 1955-2023. Nick was an energetic campaigner for creative teaching and learning and against the climate catastrophe. His death from cancer was wholly caused by neo-liberal capitalism.

Labour's Extreme Neoliberalism

Jamie Gough

Labour's Extreme Neoliberalism

Jamie Gough

Cover design: NJ Catchpole
Photo of money: Suzy Hazelwood

Published January 2025
Resistance Books
info@resistancebooks.org
www.resistancebooks.org

ISBN: 978-1-872242-31-6 (pbk)
ISBN: 978-1-872242-32-3 (e-book)

Jamie Gough has worked as a university researcher and lecturer, and in retirement continues to write. His research and writing uses a Marxist approach which spans economics, social life, politics, and the ideologies and popular consciousness which they involve. Much of his work is concerned with the tension between neoliberalism and Keynesianism and the relations between capital and labour; this is a central theme of this book.
www.jamiegough.info

CONTENTS

1 Introduction

The aim of this book is to assess the actions of the Labour government in Britain since its election in July 2024 up until January 2025, and propose an alternative. It surveys all the main economic and social policies of the government; but it has a particular focus on fiscal policy – taxation, borrowing and spending – since money is central to the relationship between capital and the state.

Keir Starmer was elected as leader of the Labour Party in 2020 on the basis of his support for Jeremy Corbyn's manifesto in the 2019 general election. But since his election, Starmer has moved continuously to the Right. Since coming to government, Labour has stuck with nearly all the policies of the 2010-24 Conservative governments. The Labour Party has thereby moved from social democracy to extreme neoliberalism. I argue that this is because it has adapted itself to the strategy of the majority of capital operating in, through and from Britain, which was consolidated during the process of Brexit. Working class organisations are now faced with struggling not only directly against capital but also against in the government. I propose that a key aspect of this struggle should be a People's Plan for Taxation which targets capital and the rich.

Section 1 analyses the government's first budget of October 2024. This budget accepted the main lines of the fiscal policy of the previous Conservative government. It ruled out any serious increase in taxation of capitalist profits and of the rich. It ensures that benefits, public services and regulation of capital will continue to decline from their already dire state.

Section 2 describes the evolution of Labour's fiscal policy since Starmer became leader: a case study of obfuscation and mystifying political spin. The Labour leadership's refusal to increase taxation of capital and the rich was allowed no discussion with the party, and there was virtually none in the media.

Section 3 criticises Labour's fiscal policy from a social-democratic standpoint. I argue that large increases in tax on the rich and corporations are eminently possible, increases which would enable a large increase in spending on public services, benefits and regulation.

Section 4 investigates Starmer's repeated claim that Labour's rightwing fiscal policy was necessary in order to win voters by showing that Labour had abandoned the 'profligate' tax and spend policies of Corbyn. But in reality, Corbyn's policies on taxation of capital and the rich are extremely popular. The large parliamentary majority won by Labour owed nothing to Starmer's new fiscal policy. Instead, Labour's promise of more austerity allowed Reform to emerge as a major player in national politics by appealing to working class discontent with living standards and public services.

In Section 5 I analyse the reasons for Labour's stampede to the right. Labour's policies in opposition and government have been developed through a myriad of consultations with representatives of capital. Labour governments always gravitate towards the majority view of capital. In 2025, this view is unprecedentedly reactionary: post Brexit, the majority of capital operating in, through and from Britain wishes for further deregulation of the labour market and of the environment, for taxes on capital and the rich to be further reduced, and to remain outside the EU Customs Union and the Single Market. Labour has adopted this strategy.

To prevent further destruction of living standards and the environment, working class organisations will have to struggle against the government on every front. In the final section of this book I argue that an important part of these struggles should be a People's Plan for Taxation to radically increase taxation of capital and the rich.

2

Labour on taxation, spending and borrowing

On 30 October 2024, Rachel Reeves presented the first Labour budget for 14 years. This set out taxation, borrowing and spending for the next four fiscal years, the duration of this parliament. It was presented by commentators of both right and left as a 'radical' return to 'tax and spend'.

It did involve a substantial increase, relative to the Tories' plans, in taxation (£40bn per year) and overall government spending (£78bn per year) than is normal in British politics (compare with total government spending of around £970bn per year). Public spending as a proportion of GDP will rise to 38%, a historic high for Britain (but much less than contemporary Germany, France, Sweden and the EU as a whole). But in relation to new taxation of corporations and the rich, which might feasibly have been undertaken, and in relation to the grossly inadequate funding of public services and benefits inherited from the Tories, it was a damp squib.

In essence, it was a continuation of the fiscal policy of the Tories over 14 years, which was itself tailored to the wishes of the majority of capital operating in, through and from Britain. In this article I examine how Labour developed this strategy over the last few years, its relation to public opinion on taxation, and the reasons for Labour's capitulation to the extreme neoliberalism of the Tories.

Budgets set out changes to the previous tax and spend plans of a year before, in this case those of the Sunak/Hunt government; they do not comment on aspects which are not to be changed. Tory fiscal policy was enclosed within self-imposed constraints: no borrowing to fund revenue spending in each year (thus ruling out even the widely accepted practice of borrowing in recessions and having a surplus in growth periods); accumulated state debt as a proportion of GDP to fall after five years. Reeves stuck with these constraints, aside from a tweak in the definition of 'debt'. While total government borrowing would be £26bn in 2025-6, there would be a surplus in the next three years, so no increase in debt over the parliament.

The Tory plan was to rule out increases in tax rates on people and business, and to carry out further real-terms reductions in spending. Reeves had promised since 2023 to not increase tax rates on 'working people' and claimed to not do so in her budget. In reality, she stuck with the Tories' freezing of income tax thresholds in nominal terms for the next three years; this is a classic 'stealth tax' increase as incomes rise with inflation many people move up into the 20% and 40% tax rate brackets. She also kept to the Tory plans for large increases in council tax in each year. So her claim to not increase taxes on 'working people' was false.

Reeves's main tax change was ostensibly to the taxation of capital: an increase in the rate of employers' national insurance contributions, raising

£26bn a year. She thus dodges any increase in tax on *profits* or on *asset values*, which are the only taxes capital really fears, and are in any sense anti-capitalist.

Employers' national insurance (NI) contributions fall disproportionately on labour intensive sectors, particularly consumer services and private sector provision of public services such as social care. Profit margins in these sectors are generally small, and employers therefore react to NI rises by holding down or reducing wages. It is estimated that 75% of the NI rise will in this way be transferred to workers in wage reductions. In social care, the great majority of which is carried out by capitalist firms and charities, and where wages are already abysmal, the rise in employers' NI threatens to close down provision in a sector that is already in a state of collapse.

Reeves's choice of NI as a tax rise on business is thus the worst option. Her only increase in taxation of profits was on North Sea oil companies: an increase from 75% to 78% on the higher-than-usual profits resulting from the Ukraine war. But she allowed all investment spending to be deducted in full in its first year, ensuring that the companies will pay little tax.

Reeves also announced small increases in taxation of the rich: through an increase in some forms of capital gains tax raising £2.5bn a year, an increase in inheritance tax yielding £2.3bn a year, and imposing VAT on private schools claimed to raise £1.7bn a year (though not accounting for the likely increase in state school enrolments). The increase in capital gains tax (CGT) falls far short of the estimated £15bn a year which would be reaped by equating the CGT rate with the highest rate of income tax. Notable was the small rise (29% to 32%) in the taxation of private equity investors (the 'carried interest' rate); there was reported to be a champagne-fuelled celebration of this leniency by private equity tycoons in their hood, Mayfair, congratulating themselves on having 'won the argument' in an earlier meeting with Reeves. The rise in taxation of the rich was thus another damp squib. Reeves promised that there will be 'no further tax rises' in the rest of the parliament.

Spending on public investment

Expenditure on 'public investment' – conventionally defined as purchase of buildings and physical infrastructures – will be £22bn a year larger than the Tories' plans, thus allowing increased spending through the National Wealth Fund on transport and energy infrastructures; green investment; subsidies to industry and R&D; and potentially on publicly-owned buildings such as schools and hospitals. Reeves reconciled this rise with sticking to the Tories' limitation of total government debt by tweaking the definition of the latter, from 'Public Sector Net Financial Liabilities' to 'Public Sector Net Debt' which includes certain publicly owned assets.

This potentially allowed her to borrow £55bn a year more than the Tories' plans, but she modestly limited the rise to £22bn a year. The small size of this fund is suggested by comparing it to the £28bn a year on green investment alone Labour had outlined in 2022 and subsequently retreated from, and the £50bn a year public investment proposed by the 2019 Labour manifesto.

Its modest size requires that the government's aims for fixed investment rely heavily on leveraging two to four times the state investment from private business. The experience of private-public partnerships over forty years indicates that investment will be dependent on sufficient profitability for the private sector, distorting its social benefits; that the investment will simply not take place; or that (as in Private Funding Initiatives for hospitals and schools) the long-term cost to the state will be many multiples of pure state investment. Regarding the implementation of these investments, the government has no plan to deal with the lack of skilled labour in the construction sector, for instance in the installation of insulation and heat pumps in housing.

Since the budget, it has become evident that there will be little or no investment purely by the state in the built environment, that is, where the private sector has no interest in being involved. A prominent instance is the repair and rebuilding of crumbling hospitals, some of which are in danger of outright collapse, and where operations are being cancelled due to building failures. Johnson's

2020 pledge of 40 new hospitals has, unsurprisingly, been a farce: barely 20 old hospitals have had any work done on them; many crumbling hospitals have not been included at all; and funding of this programme is due to end in March 2025. In January 2025 Wes Streeting announced that only five or so hospital refurbishments are to continue, leaving more than 35 in a dire state. The National Audit Office has recently estimated the backlog in repairs to public buildings as at least £49bn. The most basic and urgent investment in the built environment will not take place because of the wholly inadequate increase in the public investment fund.

Spending on public services and benefits

Reeves's increase in tax on capital and the rich, £40bn a year in total, enabled her to increase spending on public services and benefits by the same amount. Spending on public services as a whole will increase by 3.2% in real terms next year, and by even smaller amounts in subsequent years. But these increases are insufficient to maintain service levels let alone increase them; this is because productivity (use value of output per worker-hour) in public services cannot easily be increased by automation, in contrast to for example manufacturing, utilities and retailing[1]. The Institute for Fiscal Studies pointed out that a further increase in spending of £9bn a year would be needed in the second year just to maintain existing service levels.

On the spending side, military spending is to increase over five years to reach 2.5% of GDP. Only one major public service received a substantial increase: £22.6bn a year for revenue funding of the NHS. This is wholly inadequate to fill the 150,000 vacancies in the NHS, and to deal with the backlog of 7.5 million people in England waiting for hospital treatment. All other public services will be subject to the Tories' spending plans, leading to continued degradation.

Particularly hard hit are residential social care (which received a derisory £600m increase, immediately cancelled by rises in costs of £2.5bn consequent on the budget (the NHS and social care together received only an 3.2% increase); school and college education; local government (40% of local authorities in England are effectively bankrupt); the National Parks and Areas of Natural Beauty (which have been starved of funding and now face a further 20% cut); youth services and the remaining Sure Start centres; the civil service (where the Tories' cuts to staffing mean that all environmental, labour and financial regulation is a dead letter)[2]; the universities; the arts; the justice system and prisons.

These further cuts in services were compounded by the government's failure to undertake reorganisation of public services. An egregious case is residential social care of children and young people, disabled people and the elderly. This sector, which employs 2.5 million workers, is now largely owned by US private equity companies, and run as cash-cows. The result has been atrocious wages and conditions of work, gross understaffing, and barbaric non-care of residents[3]. It is blindingly obvious that the sector should be returned to local authority ownership and management; but the government refuses to do this.

The funding and organisation of benefits (transfer payments to individuals) is even worse. Reeves has continued with the Tories' plans to cut

£3bn a year or 4% from total benefit payments. There are to be no real terms increases in universal credit in real terms, nor in payments to unpaid carers (though there was a small rise in their allowed earnings).

In an extraordinary example of sado-neoliberalism, the government refused to lift the Tories' two-child limit for payment of child benefits, leaving 500,000 children in extreme poverty. Demands to end the limit came from a wide range of poverty campaigns, community groups, social democratic commentators and backbench Labour MPs; the cost would be a modest £1.7bn in the first year. Reeves removed winter fuel payments for OAPs except for the poorest which will undoubtedly lead to tens of thousands more deaths over the winter. She is to remove benefits to young people not in employment or education. Again, obvious structural reforms are refused: abolishing the five-week wait for universal credit payments; abolishing the bedroom tax; instituting a proper income for unpaid carers.

The government has used two tactics to appear to be doing something positive for public services and benefits while freezing spending on them. First, it announced 'commissions of enquiry' in a number of fields. Regarding fiscal policy, Reeves announced a commission to review public finances – but where her red lines on corporate and millionaire tax would be maintained. Health secretary Wes Streeting announced a review of the entire NHS. Another commission is to be set up on child poverty. But the causes of child poverty are known, as are solutions to it. This was transparently an attempt to distract attention from the two-child benefit policy.

The Home Secretary, Yvette Cooper, announced the creation of a 'young futures' unit, based in the Home Office, to coordinate state agencies in reducing teenage crime. This is to avoid commitment to the economic policies which could reduce teenage crime: ending poverty (a third of young people in Britain are in poverty), massively increased spending on schools, and restoring youth clubs and mentoring for young people (cut by 75% by the Tories). The aim of coordinating state agencies around teenage crime will anyway not happen – all of these agencies are grossly understaffed and already failing in their core responsibilities. Most ridiculous of all, the government has announced that it is setting up an enquiry into adult social care which will not report for three years. There have been three enquiries on this topic in the last twelve years, all of which recommended the setting up of a state funded national care service.

A second way the government seeks to avoid proper funding of services is to restructure them or to demand they reform themselves. In weirdly apocalyptic language, Starmer has said that the NHS must 'reform or die'. Streeting has said that more NHS services need to be contracted out to private health care corporations, ignoring the high costs of existing examples of contracting out. He will introduce a system of measuring the 'efficiency' and 'effort' of NHS managers by measuring the output of units under their management and sacking those who do not come up to scratch. This is the classic neoliberal management regime for public services over the last fifty years; its failures and absurdities are now well-documented.

Similarly, in December 2024, as part of his latest 'reset' of Labour's message which specified quantitative targets in five 'mission' fields, Starmer laid into the civil service, claiming that 'too many people in Whitehall are comfortable in the tepid bath of managed decline', thus requiring 'a cultural shift away from the declinist mentality'. He offered no evidence for this claim. As an explanation of the decline in public services and public administration it is fatuous: the issue is money. This attack on the civil service recapitulates the Tories' endless attacks on 'the blob', 'experts' and the 'liberal elite', and Trump's programme to clear out the Federal civil service in the name of 'efficiency'. Starmer signalled that he too is aiming to cut the number of civil servants.

Labour's other policies

The large degree of continuity with the Tories in fiscal policy is of a piece with Labour's continuation of Tory policy in other fields. Labour will not seek to re-enter the EU Customs Union nor the Single Market. Its anti-EU fervour extends to refusing an EU offer of a youth exchange scheme:

British youth are apparently doing just fine without working in Europe.

Regulation of the utilities (electricity, gas, water), telecoms, social media, monopolies and transport (rail, airports) was farcically weak under the Tories. The corporations operating these sectors, using their spatial monopolies, have extracted rent from consumers while failing to invest, which is what all private-sector monopolies do. The regulators (the various Offs) have done nothing substantial to alter this behaviour. Labour might have been expected to begin to toughen up this regulation; in the event it has done the opposite. In January 2025 Reeves called the heads of the regulators plus the Financial Conduct Authority into 10 Downing Street and instructed them to come up with five measures each which would encourage 'growth' in the economy. The intention is to further weaken constraints on the corporations and thus enable 'growth' of their profits; this will not lead to increased investment precisely because the private providers are monopolies. The head of the Competition and Markets Authority, which regulates monopolies, Marcus Bokkerink, refused to adopt Reeves's approach and was sacked. He was replaced by Doug Gurr, a former senior executive of Amazon. Amazon has a quasi-monopoly domination of internet retailing, which Gurr will presumably maintain. Reeves's extraordinary choice echoes Trump, and signals the government's prostration before US big tech, linked in particular to its ambition to make Britain a major centre of AI. (For more on the de-regulation of finance, see Section 6.)

Labour will not renationalise the water and sewage companies whose profiteering, gross lack of investment and environmental destruction are now legendary. The government claims that the cost would be too high, quoting a figure supplied by the water companies themselves. In reality, the water companies are bankrupt, or would be if they were properly regulated, and should and could therefore be nationalised at zero cost. Instead, the government will 'toughen up' regulation of investment and executive bonuses: pushing on a piece of string.

The government will continue the Tories' reactionary and environmentally destructive transport policies. Bus fares will rise from £2 to £3. There will be no increase in tax on petrol, which has decreased in real terms since 2010, nor on the obscene SUVs.

Labour has announced no new regulation of the production and sale of harmful consumer goods, services and other pursuits, for example disposable vapes, livestock farming, grouse hunting, and gambling. Egregious is the absence of policy on junk food and (related but distinct) obesity. In these areas Britain is amongst the worst in the rich countries. They not only impose ill-health on individuals, with large impacts on their ability to do wage work but cost the NHS tens of billions of pounds and rising; a recent report estimated the total annual costs at £270bn a year. The government's sole initiative here is to offer obese people, in areas with low labour-force participation, weight-loss drugs, with serious implications for their future health. Note that these failures to regulate business cannot be attributed to fiscal constraints: they would cost the government little.

The main policy on housing, of allowing the major building companies to build in the green belt, extends the Tories' policy of creating expensive, car-dependent enclaves in the wrong places with jerry-built owner-occupied housing. There is to be no public appropriation of landowners' development gain, no substantial programme for social housing, and minimal intervention into slum private rental housing.

On immigration, Labour has seamlessly continued the Tories' inhumane and illegal blocking of refugees and asylum seekers to 'stop the boats'. Starmer made this one of his five 'pledges' in the election campaign. The government has set up a new 'Border Security Force'. Labour has remained silent on the fact that 95% of immigration in 2023 was legal and that at 600,000 net immigration this was at record levels. Employers required the latter to fill vacancies, given the 9 million working-age people who are not seeking employment due, amongst other things, to ill health. The Tories, in their last years of government, had only one policy to appeal to British voters, 'stopping the boats'; Labour has continued this for the same reason, *legitimation*. The government has continued the Tories' policy of counting foreign university students as 'immigrants', and imposing expensive and restrictive visa conditions, with the aim of reducing the 'headline' rate of immigration; this has been a further blow to the universities which are already under severe financial pressure.

Labour is enacting some economic, social and environmental policies which are welcome in principle: new workers' rights, measures to improve bus services and take the railways into public ownership, the setting up of Great British Energy for a public stake in energy retailing, and the National Wealth Fund. None of these goes far enough qualitatively or quantitively. And they weigh little against the continuity with Tory strategy, including fiscal policy.

3

Labour's fiscal policy: spin without substance

For the 2017 general election, and then in a more detailed form for the 2019 election, Corbyn, MacDonnell and Long-Bailey put forward a fiscal policy which, while modest, broke decisively with the Tories' fiscal austerity. This had two main elements: a rise in taxation of corporations and the rich; and an increase in state investment funded by borrowing. The strategy makes a fundamental distinction between state current or revenue spending on the one hand and state investment spending on the other. The latter has benefits which are reaped, by citizens or by the state itself, over many years or decades. There are many grey areas between these two types of state spending, but the general idea is a useful one. There is a compelling logic for state investment spending to be funded by borrowing: repayments on the debt will be covered many times over by the benefits flowing to citizens and the state over the period of borrowing. Accordingly, the 2019 manifesto proposed to fund investment spending by borrowing.

The manifesto proposed that no one whose income was less than £80,000 a year would pay more tax (income tax, national insurance, VAT, council tax). It proposed to raise an extra £83bn a year by increasing effective tax rates on corporations (about 90% of the total) and on rich individuals (about 10%). The measures to achieve this were set out in great detail, and with cautious assumptions, in the accompanying Grey Book. Total taxation and other state revenue in 2019/20 was £840bn a year, so this would be an increase of 10%. This would enable a substantial increase in spending on public services, benefits and the civil service after nine years of Tory cuts. Regarding investment spending, the manifesto proposed £25bn a year for the Green New Deal, and £25bn a year for the National and Regional Investment Banks that would invest in industry (Gough, 2020).

Jeremy Corbyn resigned as Labour leader after the election. In the ensuing election for leader, with votes only for all party members, Keir Starmer was the candidate of the right and centre, Rebecca Long-Bailey of the left. Starmer nevertheless ran on a ten-point programme which was a summary of the manifesto, presumably because the party membership was largely Corbynite; he won with 60% of the vote, Long-Bailey receiving a third. In January 2020 Johnson signed the Withdrawal Agreement with the EU; in March came the first Covid lockdown. National political debate in the next two years was dominated by the Covid emergency and the underlying political-economic issues, including fiscal policy, were effectively buried in both national debate and within the Labour Party.

Facilitated by the lockdown, Starmer's activity was largely confined to purging the party of Corbynites through expulsions and deselections.

While the intention was clearly to junk Corbyn's programme, it was dressed up as a campaign against 'antisemitism'. A notable casualty was Long-Bailey, whom Starmer had appointed as shadow chancellor in deference to the leadership vote, who was dismissed from that post on a fatuous pretext of 'antisemitism'. She was replaced by Annaleise Dodds from the centre-left, who in turn was replaced by the reliably neoliberal Rachel Reeves, a graduate of Goldman Sachs and the Bank of England.

As the Covid emergency eased in 2022-3, Starmer felt the need to explain what Labour now stood for rather than simply criticising the government's handling of the emergency. He made a strongly hyped speech on his 'vision' for the country, T his combined vague platitudes with random micro-policy ideas; it made no mention of fiscal policy. This is a textbook case of a 'lacuna', in which the main argument is made by saying nothing about it. Unsurprisingly, this made no impact on the public: no-one was any wiser about his strategy. To rectify this failure, he made another four speeches on strategy, each one as vacuous as the one before and with as little effect.

Wes Streeting, the shadow health secretary, made congruent speeches in which he suggested tweaks to the NHS while saying nothing about its funding. Cumulatively, these speeches had an implicit message: Labour will make no substantial increase in public spending. This conservative orientation was reinforced when strikes broke out in the public sector against the wage cuts imposed over the previous 12 years, and in the private sector against wage cuts, degradation of conditions and tearing up of contracts during the Covid period. Starmer announced that Labour, as a future party of government, could have no view on these strikes, and forbade Labour MPs and councillors from appearing on picket lines. Public sector workers were to expect no wage rises from Labour. (Gough, 2021a; 2021b)

In 2023, Labour's implicit fiscal policy became explicit. Reeves came clean: there was to be no increase in taxation of the rich or of capital, and therefore no increase in public expenditure. Labour would not introduce a wealth tax, increase the highest rate of income tax, or increase the rate of tax on capital gains (the main form of remuneration for many working in the City of London) to equal the highest rate of income tax. The nominal rate of corporation tax, 25%, would not be increased, and, even more significantly, the thousand and one reliefs from corporation tax for supposed 'investments' introduced by Conservative governments would not be abolished.

To cap it all, Labour would adhere to Sunak and Hunt's pledge that government debt would decrease as a proportion of GDP by the fifth year of government. This new fiscal policy was the major plank of Starmer's new slogan, that his was a 'changed Labour Party', meaning that the party was not only purged of Corbynites but purged of Corbynism and Labour's original sin, 'tax and spend'. Labour would not increase taxes on 'you', deftly evading the distinction between ordinary people and corporations and the rich.

In place of a new fiscal policy, Starmer and Reeves presented their alternative: 'growth', presumably growth of GDP. This was to be the guiding light for a Labour government. Every action of every part of government would be directed at achieving this aim, and every policy would be subordinated to achieving it. To dramatise this aim, Starmer promised that after five years the UK would have the highest growth rate in the G7.

The seamless continuity of this new fiscal policy with the Tories' was lightly disguised with pledges to increase taxes on the rich – but in tiny ways: VAT on private school fees, increasing tax on non-doms, improving HMRC tax collection (but with no extra staff). Equally minute and random increases in spending were proposed; but each one was to be funded by ring-fenced revenue from a specific promised tax increase; thus recruitment of 3,000 more teachers was to be funded by the VAT on private-school fees. (Note in passing that, for good reasons, the British Treasury has never ring-fenced revenue from a particular source for a particular area of spending, and it never will.)

These promised micro-taxes and spends were simply rhetorical, to illustrate the overall fiscal policy: 'we will not spend on anything that is unfunded'. Implicitly, and sometimes explicitly, Reeves would compare her principle with Liz

Truss's notorious budget; we will be proper Tories, unlike the actual Tories.

In the election campaign, Labour's one and only criticism of the Tories was that they were 'incompetent'. This begs the question 'incompetent at doing what?' Labour made no criticism of the Tories' *austerity*, whether in wages and employment relations or public spending. Wage cuts and insecure employment, collapsing public services, a sadistic benefits system and catastrophic housing conditions – these were taking place in another country. I can think of no other opposition campaign in a general election where the salient features of the society were so ignored. This gap was a logical complement to Labour's fiscal policy: to mention the state of public services, benefits and infrastructure would invite the question of what Labour would do to improve these things.

After the 7th July election, Reeves continued this spin through a farcical performance of 'fiscal responsibility'. She announced she had discovered a £20bn 'black hole' in the current year's budget. The political logic of this 'discovery' was to replay in reverse the Tories' 'discovery' when they came to power in 2010 that 'Labour had bankrupted the country' by its extravagant spending (making full use of Liam Byrne's note 'There is no money'). In this vein, the Labour Leader of the Commons, Lucy Powell, on 2nd September claimed that spending cuts were required to avoid an economic crash and a run on the pound. The allusion to Liz Truss's budget is without substance: Truss's budget created extra borrowing of £45bn a year beyond expectations; and Truss would have cut taxes on the rich and corporations, whereas Reeves has plenty of scope to increase these taxes.

The main reason for Reeves's discovery of a 'black hole' was to justify Labour's fiscal policy. A half of the 'black hole' was a consequence of her having agreed to pay the recommendations of the independent public sector pay commissions. The remaining £10bn a year, 1% of public spending, is well within the margin of forecasting error and thus eminently ignorable. But Reeves chose to announce cuts to a random selection of government programmes, including old people's winter fuel allowance, hospital repair and railway investment, and IT and AI research. She sought to advertise that she has no commitment to repairing public services, increasing transfer payments, or investing in industry. This was simply softening up for her first budget in October.

For public consumption, before and after the election, Starmer repeated endlessly that the government has to stick to its fiscal rules, as if these were not his own choice but given by 'the laws of economics', nature or God. In the same vein, Reeves said, 'If we can't afford it, we can't do it', begging the question of who pays. For those familiar with the history of fiscal policy, Reeves's slogan is a direct and deliberate inversion of Keynes's dictum in the 1940s, 'Anything we can do we can afford'. She is thus announcing the abandonment of the entirety of Keynesianism, the strategy of the Labour Party from the 1940s to the late 1960s.

Starmer and Reeves's rhetoric has at the time of writing been very successful in damping down demands from trade unions, civil society and within the Labour Party for increased taxation of capital and the rich. Demands from a wide range of organisations for increased spending on aspects of the welfare state have invariably been prefaced by acknowledgement that 'public finances are tight', thus occluding any alternative tax policy and diminishing the particular demand into special pleading. In the lead up to the TUC conference, demands from the left narrowed to the single issue of pensioners' winter fuel payments.

What is so striking about this story is *the complete absence of debate* within the Labour Party and the country more widely on the most important strategy of any government. In none of their speeches did Starmer or Reeves make any *argument* concerning their policy on the annual deficit and accumulated debt; they simply asserted their policy. Nor have they made arguments to justify not increasing taxation of corporations and the rich. This is remarkable, given that for fifty years the Right has argued that such increases cause capital flight or deplete the capital available for (productive) investment – an obvious (if controversial) argument to pull off the shelf. (We shall see its falsity in the next section.)

That Starmer and Reeves have not bothered to make even this argument is presumably because they do not want to spark any debate whatsoever;

they want to maintain the idea that 'there is no alternative'. The nearest we have had is Reeves's recent claim, 'When household budgets are stretched, families have to make difficult choices. And government needs to do the same' – an analysis first put forward by Margaret Thatcher. But a capitalist state is not a household: it can choose its revenue, it can easily borrow to invest, and its spending has many positive effects on both society and the state's own finances. This lack of debate has its counterpart in the internal practices of the Labour Party: the Policy Forum and party conference have excluded any discussion of fiscal policy and in nearly all local parties, the right has used its control to prevent discussion of economic strategy by party members. This is the path that has led to the budget described above.

4

The real choices on Britain's fiscal policy

How did the Starmer-led Labour Party arrive at this far-right fiscal policy? There are, in fact, alternatives to Labour's fiscal policy. I discuss broadly social democratic, Keynesian or Corbynite alternatives. I do not discuss fully socialist alternatives here since working-class organisation and popular consciousness does not make this a feasible option for a Labour government presently (though it would be valuable propaganda; see also note 4). A number of aspects of Labour's strategy can be criticised from this point of view.

'Growth' as a solution

Over the last two decades, Britain has had the lowest growth rate of GDP among the major High Income Countries, the G7. (Note in passing that this is not true for British-headquartered capital nor for UK billionaires.) Since the Covid pandemic, Britain has had one of the lowest rates of growth among the larger group of G20 countries. If one leaves out finance and business services (around 15% of GDP), an increased rate of growth in production of useful goods and services is a necessary, though not sufficient, condition for improvements in real incomes and public spending.

But Starmer's ambition for British GDP to increase faster than the other G7 countries is pie-in-the-sky; his industrial policies are utterly insufficient to achieve this aim. The National Wealth Fund for infrastructure investment, talking to the Pension Funds about investing in Britain, and Labour's policies on training are far too weak to change the habits of capital invested in the British domestic economy. The government's pledge on growth is nothing more than evasion of the need to radically increase taxation of capital and the rich.

The social and fiscal benefits of spending

Since the 1930s, social-democratic and broadly Keynesian commentators have pointed out that state spending cannot be adequately evaluated by considering only its cost to the Treasury. Most state spending results in multiplier effects, benefits to firms and households other than the direct beneficiaries, and often also to increased income and decreased costs to the state. Starmer and Reeves have no understanding of this point. A salient example is the two-child limit on child benefit. Labour says that to abolish this limit 'cannot be afforded'. But poverty has negative impacts on children's health, mental health and cognitive abilities, and their social and technical skills. These impacts will last for their lives. The latter create additional costs to the state over decades, for example in the NHS and policing; and by lowering the skills of the labour force they create costs to the economy. But none of these disbenefits is considered by the government.

Dozens of other examples could be given of the multiple negative impacts of cuts in current state spending. Cuts in youth services, over 75% since 2010, have had multiple negative impacts on young people themselves, and led to other horrors such as the rise in gang membership and knife crime. Cuts in day care centres for the elderly and disabled have not only worsened their lives but imposed extra costs onto the NHS. A third of any increases in state benefits to the poor comes straight back to the Treasury in taxes. Cuts in the number of building inspectors have meant newly built housing is severely, often ludicrously, poorly built, with ensuing costs to the new owners. Reductions in staffing of the HMRC have meant tens of billions of pounds of uncollected taxes; in the 1990s it was calculated that each additional pound spent on HMRC staffing rendered £20 in additional tax collected.

The inability of the Labour leadership to consider these knock-on effects reflects its inability to think about society as a whole. The Labour government adopts the viewpoint of an individual or a firm in considering costs, ignoring that the state is a supremely social organisation. Labour's viewpoint is that of pure neoliberalism: 'there is no such thing as society'.

Investment versus current spending

In planning fiscal policy, Labour makes no distinction between investment and current spending, in contrast to Labour's 2019 manifesto. State investment can create benefits for society over decades; and to the extent it boosts productive facilities and productivity, it increases tax revenue to the state. It is true the boundary between investment and current spending is often moot. State spending on buildings and physical infrastructures are investments because of their physical longevity; but spending on teaching, for example, by enhancing the skills of workers in the future, also has long-lasting positive economic effects in addition to its social benefits.

Because investment spending has benefits to society and the state over decades, there is a strong justification for funding it by borrowing. The costs of borrowing (interest, capital repayment) are often more than covered by the stimulus to economic output and increased tax revenue (in addition to the capital repayment typically devalued by inflation). The government's refusal to distinguish investment and current spending reflects its inability to think about the long term, paralleling its inability to think socially.

State borrowing

The government has adopted Sunak and Hunt's rules for borrowing, albeit with a tweak in the definition of the public debt: borrowing in one year (the deficit) to be no more than 3% of GDP; and the accumulated state debt as a proportion of GDP (currently around 100%) to start to fall after five years. Labour expresses this as 'we have maxed out our credit card'. But these targets are arbitrary. A deficit above 3% in a year may be justified on multiple social and economic grounds. The state debt as a proportion of GDP is not a direct or hard constraint on a country's economic performance;

for example, it is higher in many rich countries than in Britain, and they have higher growth than Britain's. Under the post-war Atlee government, the debt stood at 250% of GDP, but the government nevertheless set up the NHS, started a large programme of council house building, introduced national insurance, and set up a systematic land-use planning system.

Moreover, the cost of the debt to the state is not dependent on its size alone but also on the interest offered on government bonds (gilt sales). The real reason for Labour's adoption of the deficit and debt rule is to put downward pressure on spending, especially on spending which benefits the general population. The deficit and debt rules are simply fetishistic representations of this class aim.

Tax on whom?

Public debate on tax in Britain is always posed as 'are you in favour of higher or lower taxes?', with no distinction between who is to be taxed; thus most people understand a policy of higher taxes to mean higher taxes *on them*. Yet the distribution of taxes between the general population on the one hand and business and the rich on the other – its class distribution – varies enormously between countries and through time in each country; it is a political choice.

Since neoliberalism's advent in the 1970s, in most high-income countries, rates of tax on capital and the rich have been reduced while those on the general population (income tax, VAT) have increased. Neoliberal authoritarian populist governments in high and low income countries have been especially active in reducing rates of tax on capital and the rich, Trump and Modi being representative. In Britain, the Tory governments in 1979-1997 and 2010-24 carried out this shift, with the Labour government of 1997-2010 failing to reverse it. Labour's discourse on tax occludes this: the distribution of tax between capital and the rich on the one hand and ordinary people on the other is not mentioned. Nor is the long-term shift of the tax burden onto the working class.

The global problem of decreasing taxation of capital and the rich

The problem of taxation of capital and the rich is by no means peculiar to Britain: it is a global problem. Effective tax rates on capital and the rich have been falling since the 1970s. Corporations have reduced their tax bills by shifting profits between countries in which they operate to those with the lowest tax rates, and leveraging tax concessions or subsidies from states by threatening to transfer production elsewhere or as a condition for new investment. Rich individuals and holders of money capital, including mafias and kleptocrats, have been able to transfer funds to tax havens and secrecy jurisdictions.

The rich have used the threat of these transfers to pressure governments to reduce tax on them. As a result, as Streeck (2017) has shown, in 1970 to 2000 the tax revenue from corporations and the rich to governments in the High Income Countries fell faster than they cut state spending, leading to deeply rooted fiscal crises in the last twenty years. While some governments (such as Britain) have reacted with further cuts to public spending, others have been unwilling or unable to do this sufficiently because of pressure from both capital and populations. This fiscal crisis is a major and intensifying contradiction of neoliberalism.

As a result, a substantial and ever-growing section of global capital, and a number of governments, argue that the rich and capital will have to pay more tax. They reason that this is the only way to stop the continued deterioration of public services and infrastructures. This deterioration inhibits productive investment, prevents the reproduction of effective labour power, harms productivity, and thus reduces profitability. It therefore increases the risk of explosions of discontent from workers and the poor.

This is a classic social-democratic argument that seeks to benefit both productive capital and better incorporate the working class. Perhaps the best-known proponents of this view are the 'Patriotic Millionaires', a group of US billionaires including George Soros who demand that they be more highly taxed. Less well-known, but more important, are a number of significant international initiatives by major states to increase taxation of capital and the rich. Three can be mentioned here.

First, since the world financial crisis of 2007-8, and particularly since the Eurozone crisis in 2010-2, the major countries in the EU – but with opposition from the UK until 2016 – have attempted to raise the rate of taxation of corporations and mobile money-capital. Germany, France and the Scandinavian countries have attempted to raise the rates of corporation tax in countries where it is low, particularly the UK, Ireland and Luxemburg; Ireland has been compelled to raise its rate from 12.5% to 15%. In 2019 the Commission attempted to introduce a directive requiring large corporations to show how much tax they pay in each member state, though this was blocked by the low-tax governments.

The EU has attempted to clamp down on tax havens, particularly Britain's Overseas Dependencies, where some rule changes have been achieved. Minimum common taxation of e-businesses, particularly the US-based big four, are being developed and have already been introduced in France. A financial transactions (Tobin) tax is in the offing.

Second, the OECD, the club of the Higher Income Countries, has negotiated an agreement, the Inclusive Framework on Base Erosion and Profit Shifting, with more than 140 governments to set a minimum tax rate on corporations of 15%, to be implemented from 2024. Average corporate tax rates had declined from 28% in 2000 to 21% in 2021; since then, the rate has stabilised, presumably as a result of the agreement. The ambition is to raise the minimum rate in the future.

Third, in 2024 the G20, chaired by the Brazilian president Lula da Silva, commissioned a report from Gabriel Zucman on the taxation of billionaires and multi-millionaires. Zucman found that the latter are currently paying an average of 0.3% per year tax on their wealth, and recommended increasing this to at least 2%, raising around $500bn a year.

A sign of the growing support for such initiatives in the international elite is that in recent years the International Monetary Fund has expressed support, arguing that this is necessary to tackle growing poverty in the Majority World. But none of these international initiatives has been supported by UK governments, and many have been actively opposed. Labour is now continuing this tradition. Reeves implicitly supports the neoliberal reduction in taxation of capital and the rich of the last forty years and rejects the Keynesian/social democratic arguments for reversing this trend.

I now briefly consider the taxes that can and should be increased in Britain. This is far from a fully costed programme but is intended simply to indicate the *scope* for taxation of capital and the rich. (For more detail, see for example the publications of the Tax Justice Network, IPPR, Prem Sikka and his research group at Sheffield University, and the CAGE centre at Warwick University.)

Taxes on capital and subsidies to capital

The principal direct tax on capital is corporation tax, levied on profits. Under the Tories, corporation tax was first reduced to 19%, then increased by Sunak to 25%. But Sunak ensured that revenue from the tax would not rise by introducing accelerated investment reliefs, whereby any type of investment by a firm was deductible from taxable profit in full in the first year, rather than spread over the period of return on the investment as previously. Labour could abolish this provision and increase the rate of corporation tax to that in the north-west countries of the EU.

Sunak's accelerated investment reliefs are but one example of the subsidies given to corporations. Kevin Farnsworth (2015) has termed these subsidies the 'corporate welfare state'. He estimated that subsidies, capital grants, tax benefits, insurance and advocacy as well as transport, energy and procurement subsidies were worth £93bn a year. Other estimates are higher. In 2024 the National Audit office found there were 341 tax breaks to corporations worth £204bn a year. In addition, the legacy costs of the 2008 bank bailouts and ongoing subsidies to banks cost an additional £35bn per year.

The subsidies to non-bank business are justified by governments and commentators as increasing investment and innovation, and thus benefiting both capital and labour; but none of these subsidies has been subject to evaluation to discover whether it has this result (Inman, 2024). The abysmal rate of productive investment and productivity increase in Britain, consistently among the lowest in the OECD, suggest that beneficial effects of corporate subsidies are minimal, and that the subsidies, like the other profits of the corporations, are distributed as dividends or in speculation. Labour could reap more than £100bn a year by culling these subsidies.

The state also subsidises banks, notably through the interest it pays on bank reserves held with the Bank of England; by reducing this by two-thirds, as suggested by a former governor of the Bank, the state could save £22bn a year (Elliott, 2024).

Another easy win from capital would be a Development Gain Tax (DGT). The base of this is the profit made by a landowner on granting of planning permission for a new development. Even in bourgeois ideology, this profit has no legitimacy since it is unearned. DGT has a long history in Labour politics: the 1945 and 1974 governments introduced it (though in both cases it was subsequently abolished by the Tories at the behest of landowners and property developers). At present, local authorities must negotiate with developers for payment of a Community Infrastructure Levy on commercial developments (offices, warehouses, etc), and to obtain some 'affordable housing' from builders of houses and flats. But local authorities are in a weak position in these negotiations, the public benefits are often dubious, and they are spatially inequitable since in poor areas the benefits are small or zero. A tax or levy going to central government would raise more and be more spatially equitable. A DGT at say 90% would raise tens of billions per year.

Taxes on the rich

Taxes on wealth, that is, the value of an individual's net assets, can reap large sums. Prem Sikka has calculated that a tax of 2% on wealth over £10m would raise £22bn a year. Inheritance Tax has a high threshold and thus falls only on the richest 1%. But the rate is low and is dodged by the richest through trusts and gifts. The government could raise the rate and prevent avoidance. The highest rate of income tax, 45%, is low by historical standards: for instance, under the Attlee government it was 98%.

Many people working in the City of London receive their income as a capital gain, the profit from buying and selling an asset, rather than as a wage. Capital gains are taxed at only 20%, compared with the top rate of income tax of 45%. An egregious case is the owners of private equity firms, whose income is taxed as capital gain under the 'carried interest' rule. (This notoriously led a private equity fund partner to brag that they paid a lower rate of tax than their cleaner.) If capital gains were taxed at 45%, the state would receive an extra £20bn a year. This is low-hanging fruit. But we have seen that Reeves raised Capital Gains Tax by only a tenth of this sum.

The rich receive tax relief on their payments into a pension fund at their (high) rate of income tax; if this was lowered to the standard rate, it would garner an estimated £20bn a year. The rate of National Insurance Contributions does not rise above an income of £150,000, making it highly regressive in this band. Instead, the rate should rise steeply with income. In addition, charging NI on unearned income could raise £8.6bn a year. Some aspects of the consumption of the rich could be taxed, not only to raise state revenue but for environmental reasons. Flights by private planes to and from British airports should be heavily taxed (or banned). The road tax on the obscene SUVs should be raised steeply, as it has been in France; Britain is presently 'a tax haven for SUVs'.

Can capital and the rich avoid increased tax?

It is widely thought, and reiterated by the Right, that contemporary 'globalisation' makes taxing corporations and the rich impossible. This is false. Regarding the rich, most of the incomes they receive are internal to Britain and therefore cannot be avoided: profits from the sale of land and property, most capital gains, legacies. These are not avoidable even if the recipient moved abroad. Regarding taxation of personal wealth, this can be avoided by changing their supposed place of residence; but when a wealth tax was introduced in Norway the number emigrating was tiny. The residence of the rich is strongly rooted in place by their social and economic life.

Regarding taxation of corporations, all the measures mentioned concern profits made within Britain. The main geographical obstacle to taxing them is corporations' practice of transfer pricing between subsidiaries in different countries to locate profits in the lowest-tax jurisdictions; outputs from one subsidiary input to another can have their price artificially changed, and a license fee charged for the use of a patent, product or service. But these transfer prices are not mysterious, but determinate economic prices which can be discovered by a well-staffed and skilled tax office. In Britain, the barrier to this has been the lack of will of the senior officers of the HMRC, and lying behind this, of governments.

Under Blair, the head of HMRC David Hartnett, declared that the organisation was 'business friendly', that is, that corporations would be allowed to state their taxable profits in Britain with no investigation. Additionally, corporations have been simply let off what they owed. After a long investigation, HMRC had a cast-iron case to tax

Vodafone £6bn for its profits on the 2000 acquisition of Mannesmann; this was turned into a £1bn bill by David Hartnett. Thus the crucial element in increasing taxation of corporate profits is political direction by the government, appointing suitable leadership to the HMRC, and increasing its staffing by experienced and skilled investigators.

It is unlikely that the government will take this path. It has set up a panel of four experts to advise on tax avoidance. One is Sir Edward Troup, a corporate lawyer and former head of HMRC who wrote in 1999 that 'taxation is legalised extortion' (Guardian, 2024). So corporate tax avoidance will continue.

Taking this together, one can conclude that there is scope for increased tax revenue from capital and the rich of the order of £100-150bn in the first year and over £200bn a year thereafter. If we recall that Labour's 2019 manifesto set out a carefully and conservatively costed rise in tax revenue from these sources of £83bn a year (in the 'Grey Book'), this target is not particularly ambitious. But it can enable a large and desperately needed injection of revenue funding into the public services, including through local government, and into benefits. Borrowing for investment in the narrow sense of building, for example social housing, the repair of hospitals and schools, and the railways, can also be greatly expanded, with positive multipliers in tax revenue.

Given the feasibility of this alternative fiscal policy, why have Starmer and Reeves stuck to the Tories' rules? Before analysing this question, I will consider a reason repeatedly cited by the Labour leadership and its supporters in the media: a pledge of fiscal austerity was necessary to win the election, and Labour's landslide victory shows the wisdom of this pledge.

5

Was austerity necessary to win the election?

In 2023 the Labour leadership started to speak of a 'transformed' or 'changed' or 'new' Labour Party; in 2024 this rhetoric was a major part of Labour's electoral campaign. This was to say: 'we have got rid of Corbyn and Corbynism'; we have got rid of Corbyn's antisemitism and his lack of patriotism (Starmer draped himself in union jacks at every opportunity); but most importantly, we have dumped Corbyn's fiscal policy of increasing both taxation and spending. The Labour leadership claimed that it was Corbyn's 'tax and spend' policy that lost Labour the 2019 election, and that their new, restrictive fiscal policy, was essential to win voters to Labour.

Since the election, Starmer and his acolytes have repeatedly claimed that their embrace of fiscal austerity accounts for their large majority, and that 'the public now trusts Labour with the economy'. Starmer takes every opportunity to make the link between defeating Corbynism, winning the election, and his new fiscal policy. Thus at the TUC conference on 11 September 2024 he claimed that 'turning around public finances will be hard. But just as we had to do the hard graft of change in our party, now we have to roll up our sleeves and change our country'.

These claims are empirically false. First, Corbyn's fiscal policy was and remains very popular. Second, Labour's large majority in 2024 was in no way due to its austerity fiscal policy; rather, it was due to the right-wing vote being split between the Conservatives and Farage's Reform Party.

Corbyn's policy of increased taxation of capital and the rich enabling a large increase in revenue spending had large support in the electorate. Opinion polls consistently show a large majority of voters think that the rich should be taxed more; this is true even of a majority of Tory voters. Polls also show large majorities for an increase in spending on public services.

Corbyn's fiscal policy, a key part of his call for an end to austerity, played a major role in the extraordinary success of the Labour Party in the 2017 general election. Starting from a low level of support when Teresa May called the election, during the election campaign Labour's support increased rapidly on the basis of its programme, and the party came within 10 seats of winning the election. This was despite the brazen sabotage of Labour's campaign by the party's Right and its apparatus. This policy advantage over the Conservatives was disguised in the 2019 general election by Boris Johnson's winning hand, 'Get Brexit done', which had enormous appeal after 3.5 years of non-negotiations with the EU, parliamentary farce, and effective suspension of governance of British economy and society. The Labour Party campaign was weakened by adoption of a convoluted and absurd commitment to hold a further referendum on EU membership; this position was largely the work of one Keir Starmer, shadow secretary on Brexit. Corbyn made a number of serious tactical errors. But the disastrous result of the vote for Labour was in no way due to voters' opposition to Labour's fiscal policy. (For a detailed analysis, see Gough, 2020.)

The Labour leadership claims that its austerity fiscal policy accounts for Labour's landslide win of the 2024 election. This is a wholly implausible argument. Let us look at the results of the 2019 and 2024 elections.

Proportion of the total vote in the 2019 and 2024 general elections, by party (%)

	2019	2024
Conservatives	43.6	24
Labour	32.2	34
Liberal Democrat	11.5	12
Scottish National Party	3.9	3
Brexit/ Reform	2.0	14
Green	2.7	7
Other	4.1	6
Conservatives + Brexit/ Reform	45.6	38
Labour + LD + SNP + Green	50.3	56

The vote share of Labour hardly increased from 2019 to 2024. A half of the increase was accounted for by a higher vote for Labour in Scotland at the expense of the SNP. The picture is even worse in terms of number of votes per elector, since turnout (proportion of electors voting) fell from 67.3% in 2019 to 59.7% in 2024. Whereas 21.7% of electors voted Labour in 2019, only 20.3% did so in 2024. On this measure, Starmer's offer was significantly less popular than Corbyn's. The very large drop in turnout between the elections, of 7.6%, suggests that the electorate was hardly enthused by Labour's offer of 'change' and 'greater competence'.

If we compare vote share for the Right (Conservatives + Brexit/Reform) with the Centre-Left (Labour + LD + SNP + Green) there was a 6-7% point swing from the former to the latter. But only a small part of this swing was due to Labour winning a greater share: the majority of the swing was due to the Green vote share increasing by 2.5 times.

The seats won by Labour massively increased from 2019 to 2024. In 2019 the Tories achieved a majority of 80 seats, whereas in 2024 Labour reaped a majority of 158. This difference had one cause: the Right vote was split between the Tories and Farage's Reform Party. Farage increased his party's vote share from 2% in 2019 to an astonishing 14% in 2024; Reform's vote was 58% of the Conservative's. Reform's popularity was, for the most part, based on its open xenophobia and racism, focused on, but not limited to, asylum seekers crossing the channel in boats. It also promised to stand up for old-fashioned masculinity, 'letting lads be lads', riffing off Andrew Tate; this presumably accounts for the alarming fact that as many 18-30 year-old *men* voted for Reform as for Labour.

Reform also put forward various economic benefits for working class people (wholly unfunded of course). The Reform vote deprived the Tories of most of the seats they had won in the North and Midlands of England in 2019, and then some. (Reform won only four seats because its vote was evenly spread across England.) The reduction in Tory seats by Reform voters, and the (successfully targeted) Lib Dem vote in the South of England, wholly accounts for Labour's majority.

The vote for Reform owes much to the Tories' central, in fact only, political campaign in the last few years, that against asylum seekers. But it was also caused by Labour's election campaign. Starmer continued the Tories' hostility to asylum seekers; he made setting up a 'Border Security Command' (note the military terminology) one of his five 'pledges' in the election campaign; he has refused to set up feasible avenues for people to apply for asylum in their own countries. Labour made no direct criticisms of Reform during the campaign, and ordered Labour's candidate in Clacton, who had carried out an effective campaign against Farage, to switch his campaigning elsewhere.

Most importantly, Labour presented no economic and fiscal programme to address the economic discontents and resentments of people who voted Reform, overwhelmingly working and lower-middle class (see also Gough, 2017). This is another measure of Labour's failure to address the dire state of employment and public services. The xenophobic riots which broke out a month after the election, inspired and legitimated by Reform's vote, were thus caused not only by the Tories but also by the Labour Party.

Two months after the election, the government's popularity had plummeted. The government had an approval rating of only 23% (compared with 68% for Blair early in his government); Starmer's approval rating is minus 16% (compared with Blair's +65%) (Simon Jenkins in *The Guardian*, 10 Sept 24). Whereas Starmer has obtained the acquiescence of the majority of the unions, centre left politicos and movements (section 2), the public is evidently unconvinced of his austerity programme.

We can conclude that Starmer's claim that his race to the Right won him the election and is a popular mandate is false; in fact, the opposite is the case.

6

Why did Labour adopt this fiscal policy?

If Labour's fiscal policy is not explained by the infeasibility of taxing capital and the rich, and was not required to win the election, then what explains it? We can start with agency and proceed to structure. Neither Starmer nor Reeves has any background in the labour movement broadly conceived – trade unions, popular campaigns, progressive movements, community politics and local government. Starmer was a lawyer before becoming an MP. Reeve's career was in the City, including Goldman Sachs and the Bank of England. This has inclined her to the current strategies of the British and international capitalist class.

I noted in section 3 that the Labour leadership has allowed no discussion of its fiscal policy within the party, and has abstained from discussion on it in parliament, civil society and the media. But, as recounted in detail by Peter Geoghegan (2024), the leadership has nevertheless been discussing economic and fiscal policy with great intensity – but in private. Shadow ministers have been in conclave with key representatives of capital: lobbyists, the big four accountancy/management firms, seconded staff from corporations, and Tony Blair and Peter Mandelson. At 2023 party conference, Starmer told a 'business forum' that 'if we do come into government, you will be coming into government with us.' Jim Murphy, former Scottish Labour leader and now lobbyist, predicted that this will be 'the first private sector government in Labour's history' (Geoghegan, 2024: 10)

Since it became evident in 2022 that the Tories would be defeated at the next election, capital and its representatives have been flocking to commune with shadow ministers, in the expectation not only of influencing policy but obtaining benefits and contracts from future ministers. Britain has the largest number of lobbyists of any state apart from the US and EU; they are an integral part of how Westminster works. The big four 'accountancy' corporations are all-purpose advisors to corporations on everything from production, organisation and marketing to tax and ownership structures to finance. They thus have a unique position as gatherers of the views of every sector of capital. Since the Blair/Brown government, the big four have not merely given technical advice to government departments but have increasingly been contacted to develop policy.

Industrial, service and financial corporations have seconded staff, free of charge, to help shadow ministers in the development of policy, and have donated to the party and individual MPs. The outsourcing multinationals with existing contracts to the British state play a major role in advising Labour in their fields of operation, reinforcing the Starmer-Reeves admiration for contracting out and privatising of public services. An egregious example is the appointment of Alan Milburn as a director in the DHSC; since his stint as health secretary under Blair, Milburn has acted as consultant and fixer to US private health and social care corporations. A number of extreme-right US billionaires have been influential. The consultancy/advocacy firms ('foundations') set up by Tony Blair and Peter Mandelson have had especially close relations with the shadow cabinet; Blair and Mandelson, the *eminences grises* of the Labour Party under Starmer, are the most authoritative and influential advisors.

These networks suggest a possible element of explanation for the Labour leadership's fiscal policy. But they beg further questions: why has the leadership privileged advice from representatives of capital; and what advice do the latter give? To answer these questions, we need to consider the nature of the Labour Party as a party, and the balance of class forces brought in by the Brexit process.

Social democracy and the Labour Party

Since its inception Labour has been a social democratic party (in the post-1914 sense). Social democratic parties offer something to the working-class conservatives do not. They do so through governing the state or parts of it; they do not take part in or build the struggles of the working class against capital (trade unions, residents' group, progressive campaigns) but remain 'neutral' in the name of 'governing for the nation'. But in capitalism, the state, lacking control of the means of production (physical, financial) can only act with the backing, or at least the acquiescence, of the majority of capital operating in the given territory.

Sections of capital which directly employs labour ('productive capital') sometimes support the improvement of the wages, working conditions, health and education of workers and improvements in the built and natural environment, as a way of enhancing cooperation of workers with capital and thus improving productivity and profitability; money capital, especially in its most liquid and mobile forms, is generally hostile to these concessions. During long waves of strong growth and high profitability such as the 1948-73 boom the views of productive capital can predominate. But in periods of low growth and low profitability, such as the interwar period and from 1973 to the present, the viewpoint of money capital predominates: wages must be held down and labour intensified in order to raise the rate of profit.

This acute sensitivity to the views of the majority of capital in a particular period can be seen in the history of Labour governments (Hazeldine, 2024). The 1924 and 1931 Labour-led governments attacked working class living standards, the strategy of capital in the inter-war depression. The 1945 Atlee government brought in a large expansion of the welfare state because the majority of capital saw this as necessary to head-off discontent after the war and to rebuild the productive economy (while at the same time pursuing a reactionary-imperial foreign policy). The Keynesian-progressive programmes on which the 1964 and 1974 Wilson governments were elected were abandoned in favour of austerity when 'the markets' demanded it (1966) or when capital as a whole moved towards neoliberalism (1976). The Blair-Brown government in 1997-2010 carried out some repair to public services, but made no change in Thatcher's anti-trade union laws and failed to reverse the inequitable distribution of income wrought by the Tories. Labour actively enhanced the dominance of the internationalised financial capital over the British economy and bailed it out after the 2008 crash, thus bequeathing a large state debt. They failed to point out who was culpable for the crash, and thus laid the basis for 14 years of Tory rule. In following the wishes of capital, the Starmer-Reeves government, post-Corbyn, is thus reverting to type.

The demands of capital

So what are the demands on the British state of the majority of capital in 2024? These have been given a new direction by the process of Brexit (see Gough, 2021c; Gough and Kirby, 2021; Gough, forthcoming). The project of Brexit was inaugurated by Alternative Investment Finance (hedge funds, private equity, asset management) in London, in response to restrictions on its operations enacted by the EU in 2011 (Benquet and Bourgeron, 2022). It was opposed by capital in manufacturing and cultural industries operating within

Britain, and by the retail and investment banks. However, after the Leave campaign won the 2016 referendum, the major companies in these sectors were able to transfer a large part of their operations to factories on the continent (manufacturing transnationals) and to other financial centres in the EU (investment banks); their opposition to a hard Brexit was thereafter tepid.

From 2016 three major sectors of capital which had not strongly participated in the referendum realised that they could benefit from a hard Brexit. First, for international money capital (ex-Soviet, Gulf, Chinese; oligarchical, kleptocratic, mafia) London is the world's major money-laundering system, channelling their money into the secrecy jurisdictions of the British Overseas Dependencies and others, with the help of a coterie of financial and legal firms in the City (Bullough 2019; 2023). As we saw in section 3, the EU, led by Germany and France, has long sought to raise the rate of corporation tax across and the block and to severely restrict or close down the operations of the British Overseas Dependencies in particular.

This enormous but invisible sector of world capital accordingly used its myriad connections in British politics to support a hard Brexit. Second, a large proportion of British-headquartered capital operates entirely outside the EU: the major construction companies building cities in the Middle and Far East; the imperial mining, oil, food and tobacco corporations; some manufacturers such as Dyson. Their interest was, again, in preserving the low effective rates of corporate taxation in Britain. Third, 70% of British GDP consists of firms selling services within Britain: the utilities, rail and bus companies, construction, hospitality, leisure and retail, and consumer finance. These do not trade with the EU. All have an interest in continued low effective corporation tax. Most have an interest in avoiding EU environmental and labour market regulations, which have been generally more stringent than indigenous British regulation. This sector too swung behind a hard Brexit.

This constellation of capitalist interests explains the main lines of the Labour government's strategy. First, it explains why Starmer has rejected any moves to re-join the Customs Union and the

Single Market, despite pleas by social-democratic/Keynesian commentators, smaller exporters, food and plant exporters and importers, the cultural industries and the universities. Second, it explains why Labour's improvements to workers' rights are so limited. Third, it explains why Labour has failed to propose any new substantial environmental regulation, and in fact has moved to further weaken it (land use planning, North Sea oil). Fourth, it explains the November announcement by Reeves that she intends to remove many or all of the restrictions on financial speculation that were introduced after 2008, in order to allow greater 'risk taking'. Connectedly, members of the royal family, following a hundred-year-old role, have been dispatched on a charm offensive to the Saudi, Bahrain and Gulf dictators to secure a new trade agreement and to ensure the continued flow of their money capital through the City of London.

Finally, and most relevant to my focus in this book, the post-Brexit constellation of capitalist interests explains why Labour refuses to increase corporate taxation and taxation of the rich. The only sectors with a strong interest in sustaining such taxation are those that depend on well-reproduced labour power – hence well-funded public services and reasonable-cost housing, and which depend on efficient physical infrastructures – which require substantial public funding. Such sectors of capital are confined to some sectors of manufacturing, high-tech engineering such as power stations, and the cultural industries. (Public services require well-reproduced labour power, but they are largely non-capitalist and thus have no political weight with the government.)

Sectors such as finance and software writing use skilled labour power, but this is adequately reproduced by the existing society, largely through high wages. All other sectors of capital either use low-skill, replaceable labour power (services within Britain), or produce abroad. Conversely, we have seen that all other sectors of capital other than manufacturing and cultural industries have an interest in low taxation of corporations (and of multi-millionaires, who are small corporations in the own right). This interest in low corporate taxation is true of capitalist services operating with Britain, and of British-headquartered corporations producing abroad. It is most strongly true of overseas money capital invested through London and its enablers in London: for them, the low effective taxes on capital and the continued existence of the British-controlled overseas tax havens are *an essential condition* to their sending their money through London.

Putting these interests together, we see that the totality of capitalist interest – the government's guiding light – is to maintain and even enhance the low taxation of corporations and the very rich. This key feature of the budget is thus explained.[1]

7

What should be the response?

What should be the response of the left to the government's capitulation on tax? Since taxation grew in the early twentieth century, the broad labour movement, particularly the trade unions, have paid remarkably little attention to tax policy – who or what is taxed and at what rates. Tax policy was left to the Labour Party and Labour governments. A notable exception was the explosive collective resistance to Thatcher's poll tax in 1988-90, which played a large roll in her toppling by the Tory grandees and the substitution of council tax by John Major. But the depth and radicalism of the anti-poll tax movement was a function of the extremism and adventurism of the poll tax – the richest and the poorest were to pay the same in absolute terms (pounds). And the movement was purely negative; it didn't result in positive proposals for the system of local (let alone national) taxation. Its result was council tax which was highly regressive and more regressive than the domestic rates which applied up until 1988.

One might argue that another partial exception to the grassroots labour movement's abstention on tax was the Corbyn-McDonnell tax proposals in the 2019 manifesto: while they were written by Labour Party politicians, they were based on the massive participation in the party of leftists fed up with austerity and reflected a radical consciousness of millions hostile to corporate and private wealth. This suggests that there is a strong basis in the present for developing a long-term popular campaign for radically increased taxation of capital and the super-rich. John McDonnell has instigated some discussions of this topic since 2020; but he, and the Socialist Campaign Group of Labour MPs, have kept their heads below the parapet and are too fragmented to lead any popular movement.

Short of the formation of a new socialist or broad left class struggle party (around which there are currently some discussions), the best hope for developing a popular movement on this topic is from the trade unions and grass roots campaigns in association with MPs from the Socialist Campaign Group, the Green Party and the left independent MPs. With advice from the Tax Justice Network and sympathetic academics and imaginatively publicised in the style of Lions Led by Donkeys, this could be a powerful component of emerging working-class resistance to, and influence on, the Labour government.

Such a campaign could also help to reduce the attraction of the increasingly popular Reform Party (which, as we have seen, has been substantially the fault of the Labour Party). A People's Plan for Taxation provides an alternative to Reform's reactionary economic and social policies; and the demand to tax the corporations and the rich points the finger at Reform's super rich and corporate backers.

NOTES

1. The increase in spending in real terms is adjusted for (anticipated) inflation. Leaving aside oil and gas prices (fluctuating, and with a large element of rent), inflation is determined by price rises across the whole of capitalist production of goods and services. In most of these, there are regular substantial increases in productivity as a result of mechanisation. These are generally not available in public services.

2. The under-staffing of the national and local civil service and of regulatory bodies has received very little attention in public and political discourse, even of the left. But cuts to the civil service have resulted in chaotic, inefficient or in some cases non-existent delivery of (supposed) government policies. For example, during Covid the grossly chaotic,

corrupt and wasteful programmes of purchase of PPE and of grants and subsidies to firms was in a large part due to shortage of national and local civil servants. There is a myriad of fields of regulation by national or local government or by quasi-independent regulatory bodies: wages, conditions and health and safety at work, product quality and safety, care homes and hospitals, industrial pollution, waste disposal, rented housing, water and sewage, energy, public transport, building, car behaviours (MOTs, speeding) and so on. These have been built up over a hundred years, largely with the aim of benefiting the public and the environment (though also preventing under-cutting of good firms by bad). But due to cuts in staffing, not a single one of these areas of regulation now functions, and many are laughably ineffective. One of the reasons for the glacially slow administration of compensation to victims of government misconduct (contaminated blood, Windrush, post offices, and so on) is the lack of staff. This will continue until there is a large increase in the number of civil servants.

3. Many children in care are now located at great distance from their families and friends, many in unsupervised B&Bs, caravans and tents, and fed little more than milk and biscuits. Yet local authorities pay the providers £50,000 to £500,000 a year per child.

4. At a higher level of historical abstraction, that of capitalism in general, Reeves's policy is a fetishisation of Value. Value is the reified representation of socially necessary labour time. The Value in question here is not that of commodities but of capital as an asset, 'fictitious capital' which develops out of capitalist production. The fundamental dynamic of capitalism is the need for fictitious capital to expand continuously and indefinitely. In the case of fiscal policy (a) capital cannot be reduced by taxation since it demands to be increased, and (b) the state annual deficit and accumulated debt demand

to be reduced. This is a critique of Labour's fiscal policy from the standpoint of socialism.

REFERENCES

Benquet, M. and Bourgeron, T. (2022) *Alt-Finance: how the City of London bought democracy*, London: Pluto Press

Bullough, O. (2019) *Moneyland: why thieves and crooks now rule the world and how to take it back*, London: Profile Books

Bullough, O. (2023) *Butler to the World: how Britain became the servant of tycoons, tax dodgers, kleptocrats and criminals*, London: Profile Books

Elliott, L. (2024) Tip for Reeves: black hole can be filled overnight if we stop subsidising banks, *Guardian*, 5 August

Farnsworth, K. (2015) *The British Corporate Welfare State: public provision for private businesses*,

Sheffield: Sheffield Political Economy Research Institute

Geoghegan, Peter (2024) Labour and the lobbyists, *London Review of Books*, 15 August

Gough, J. (2017) Brexit, xenophobia and left strategy now, *Capital and Class* 41 (2) 366-372

Gough, J. (2020) Why the Labour Party lost the British 2019 general election: social democracy versus neoliberalism and the Far Right, *Class, Race and Corporate Power,* 18 (2)

http://www.jamiegough.info/sites/default/files/downloads/Why%20Labour%20lost%20the%20election_0.pdf

Gough, J. (2021a) Starmer's capitulation to the Tory budget, and what the left should propose.

https://jamiegough.info/starmers-capitulation-to-the-tory-budget-and-what-the-left-should-propose/

Gough, J. (2021b) Mr Starmer's sweet nothings. https://jamiegough.info/mr-starmers-sweet-nothings

Gough, J. (2021c) The capitalist interests behind Brexit, *Red Pepper*, March

Gough, J. and Kirby, J. (2021) How neoliberal populists serve capital: the business interests behind Brexit, York Left Consortium https://marxiststudies.blog.yorku.ca/2021/03/how-neoliberal-populists-serve-capital-business-interests-behind-brexit-gough-kirby/

Gough, J. (forthcoming) *Understanding Brexit: the overlooked role of business*

Guardian, The (2024) Editorial: The £5bn question that is unlikely to be answered by a tiny coterie of insiders, 11 April

Hazeldine, T. (2024) Neo-Labourism in the saddle, *New Left Review*, 148: 5-22

Inman, P. (2024) Labour's first job is to fix the financial plumbing, *Observer*, 8 September

Streeck, W. (2017) After capital's revolt: an interview with Wolfgang Streeck. https://www.versobooks.com/en-gb/blogs/news/3248-after-capital-s-revolt-an-interview-with-wolfgang-streeck

ABOUT RESISTANCE BOOKS

RESISTANCE BOOKS is a radical publisher of internationalist, ecosocialist, and feminist books. Resistance Books publishes books in collaboration with the International Institute for Research and Education (www.iire.org), and the Fourth International (www.fourth.international). For further information, including a full list of titles available and how to order them, go to the Resistance Books website.

info@resistancebooks.org
www.resistancebooks.org

Also in the ACR pocket book series

Resisting Trumpism
Daniel Tanuro, Paris Wilder, Gilbert Achcar, Simon Hannah & Echo Fortune

EcoSocialist Revolution: A Manifesto
AntiCapitalist Resistance

Making Sense of Russia's Invasion of Ukraine
Paul Le Blanc

Capitalist China and Socialist Revolution
Simon Hannah

Ecosocialism Not Extinction
Allan Todd

Stalinist Realism and Open Communism: Malignant Mirror or Free Association
Ian Parker

Radical Psychoanalysis and Anti-capitalist Action
Ian Parker

Mind Fuck:
The Mass Psychology of Creeping Fascism
Neil Faulkner

Alienation, Spectacle and Revolution:
A critical Marxist essay
Neil Faulkner

Why We Need Anti-capitalist Resistance
Simon Hannah

ABOUT ACR

AntiCapitalist Resistance is an organisation of revolutionary socialists. We believe red-green revolution is necessary to meet the compound crisis of humanity and the planet.

We are internationalists, ecosocialists, and anticapitalist revolutionaries. We oppose imperialism, nationalism, and militarism, and all forms of discrimination, oppression, and bigotry. We support the self-organisation of women, Black people, disabled people, and LGBTQI+ people. We support all oppressed people fighting imperialism and forms of apartheid, and struggling for self-determination, including the people of Palestine.

We favour mass resistance to neoliberal capitalism. We work inside existing mass organisations, but we believe grassroots struggle to be the core of effective resistance, and that the emancipation of the working class and the oppressed will be the act of the working class and the oppressed ourselves.

We reject forms of left organisation that focus exclusively on electoralism and social-democratic reforms. We also oppose top-down 'democratic centralist' models. We favour a pluralist organisation that can learn from struggles at home and across the world.

We aim to build a united organisation, rooted in the struggles of the working class and the oppressed, and committed to debate, initiative, and self-activity. We are for social transformation, based on mass participatory democracy.

www.anticapitalistresistance.org
info@anticapitalistresistance.org

www.ingramcontent.com/pod-product-compliance
Ingram Content Group UK Ltd.
Pitfield, Milton Keynes, MK11 3LW, UK
UKHW020810070325
455964UK00015B/204

9 781872 242316